Something Missing From This World

Something Missing
from This World

CONTEMPORARY YAZIDI POETRY

EDITED BY
Bryar Bajalan, Alana Marie Levinson-LaBrosse,
Shook, and Zêdan Xelef

DALLAS, TEXAS

Phoneme Media, an imprint of Deep Vellum Publishing
3000 Commerce St., Dallas, Texas 75226
deepvellum.org · @deepvellum

Deep Vellum is a 501c3 nonprofit literary arts organization founded in 2013 with the mission to bring the world into conversation through literature.

Support for this publication has been provided in part by grants from the National Endowment for the Arts, the Texas Commission on the Arts, the City of Dallas Office of Arts and Culture, the Communities Foundation of Texas, and the Addy Foundation.

Paperback ISBN: 978-1-64605-347-6 | Ebook ISBN: 978-1-64605-359-9

LIBRARY OF CONGRESS CATALOGING-IN-PUBLICATION DATA

Names: Bajalan, Bryar, editor. | Levinson-LaBrosse, Alana Marie, editor. | Shook, David (Poet) 1986- editor. | Xelef, Zêdan, 1995- editor.
Title: Something missing from this world : contemporary Yazidi poetry / edited by Bryar Bajalan, Alana Marie Levinson-LaBrosse, Shook, and Zêdan Xelef.
Description: First U.S. edition. | Dallas, Texas : Phoneme Media/Deep Vellum, 2024.
Identifiers: LCCN 2024016185 (print) | LCCN 2024016186 (ebook) | ISBN 9781646053476 (trade paperback) | ISBN 9781646053599 (ebook)
Subjects: LCSH: Yezidi poetry, Arabic--21st century. | Yezidi poetry, Arabic--21st century--Translations into English. | Yezidi poetry, Kurdish--21st century. | Yezidi poetry, Kurdish--21st century--Translations into English.
Classification: LCC PJ7694.E3 S66 2024 (print) | LCC PJ7694.E3 (ebook) | DDC 892.7/1708891597--dc23/eng/20240625
LC record available at https://lccn.loc.gov/2024016185
LC ebook record available at https://lccn.loc.gov/2024016186

Cover design by Pablo Marín/Verbum Media
Interior layout and typesetting by KGT

Dedicated to the memory of Minoka
Ji Minoka re

Contents

Introduction

This anthology gathers poetry written by eleven Yazidi poets who survived the genocide that began on August 3rd, 2014. Following the withdrawal from their traditional homeland by the Iraqi Armed Forces and the Kurdish Peshmerga, the Islamic State seized control of the predominantly Yazidi city of Shingal, named for the holy mountains five kilometers to its north, and began summarily executing Yazidis. Two hundred thousand Yazidis fled the city and surrounding areas, seeking safety in the neighboring Kurdistan Region of Iraq, Syria, and Turkey. Some fifty thousand fled to the Shingal mountains, a one-hundred-kilometer-long range the Yazidis consider sacred. Surrounded by Islamic State militants, many, including several of the poets in this volume, faced starvation and dehydration, and several hundred children, elderly, and disabled Yazidis died before the Kurdish People's Protection Units (YPG) and Kurdistan Workers' Party (PKK) broke the Islamic State's siege on the mountain six days later. According to United Nations estimates, that August the Islamic State massacred five thousand Yazidi men and kidnapped an estimated seven thousand Yazidi women and girls, who were forced into sex slavery. Over four hundred thousand Yazidis were displaced into the camps where many still live today.

Nothing about this anthology was inevitable. In fact, from some perspectives, it is a miracle. This constellation of writers and their intersecting life stories could easily lend itself to the type of epic storytelling the Yazidi have practiced for centuries. Its story could begin with any one of its contributors, all of whom worked diligently to locate themselves as students, poets, and humans after surviving the 2014 genocide. As editor, translator, and poet Zêdan Xelef says, "We are all characters in one another's stories." Tracing Zêdan 's story will lead us to them all.

In late 2014, Zêdan stood in line for four hours, petitioning for access to student housing at the University of Duhok in the Kurdistan Region of Iraq (KRI). Only three months earlier, the Islamic State's genocidal campaign against the Yazidi people had displaced Zêdan from their village in the shadow of Shingal Mountain, in the northwest corner of present-day Iraq, to the Chammishkko Camp for Internally Displaced People (IDPs). The first in their village to attend the University of Duhok, Zêdan could not find the four additional roommates required to be assigned a room. The Student Housing Administration dismissed Zêdan by rote: "Go post on Facebook." So Zêdan was squatting in the sun in front of the History Department to do just that when Ameer, a fellow student from Bashiqa that they had met a week ago at registration, tapped them on the shoulder. "Don't post," he said, when he heard what was happening. "I have another two and we're looking for one more. We're all Yazidis, which is good because the Muslim students won't live with you. They won't eat our food. Plus, we have been waiting so long, and we're close to the front of the line again. Join us and you won't have to stand in line again." Zêdan didn't hesitate.

The four young Yazidis secured a room in downtown Duhok above a street jammed with shwarma shops, bookshops, mechanics, and tire shops, their wares stacked in leaning towers and haphazard piles. So many tires clogged the street that the new friends would joke, "What do Kurds do? Use their tires for a year then burn them to celebrate Nawroz?" But at least there were a few liquor stores as well. The building had no elevator. They walked six flights of stairs up to the room, which was entirely empty. The entire dorm floor shared a kitchen, its sink piled high with dirty dishes. The windows overlooked the headquarters of the local ruling political party: a complex filled with gunmen and military personnel just a few kilometers from Mosul, then the hottest frontline with the Islamic State. Only two weeks into the semester, all but Ameer and Zêdan had dropped out of school to ride the migration wave toward Europe, on lifeboats in the Mediterranean or on foot through the forests of Hungary and Belarus. A few weeks later, Ameer left with his family. For three months, Zêdan lived in that room on their own, speaking with no one.

Then one day, in the shared kitchen, Asaad, a Yazidi student from Sîba, approached them. "Brother, my roommates and I have been debating. They think you don't look Yazidi, but I think you are from this one time I overheard you on the phone. Am I right?" Zêdan confirmed they were, in fact, Yazidi, and Asaad invited them to his place to meet his roommates. When Zêdan entered the room, before they even said hi to anyone, they found a copy of Ahmed Saadawi's *Frankenstein in Baghdad*. Then Gustav Le Bon's *Psychology of Crowds*. As they wondered who owned these books, Jaff—a poet included in this anthology—stepped up and introduced himself. The two of them began visiting bookstores, sometimes sitting on a bench after buying groceries to read and share poems with each other.

Jaff knew Murad and Sarmad, two other poets included in this anthology, who introduced themselves with a bottle of whiskey they had lugged up the six flights of stairs. "Quite a Sisyphean life you live up here," Sarmad said. Whiskey, poems, and a new apartment they all shared cemented the friendships. Soon Emad came to visit, toting another whiskey bottle like an entrance fee. Unlike the others, who all read the poems they'd written from their phones, Emad, Sarmad teased, was "old school," and pulled his printouts from a jacket pocket. The group began to meet regularly, encouraged, too, by Murad's efforts to organize Yazidi students on campus.

During the summer they met on the eastern bank of the Tigris, where that river meets the Xabûr, just a few kilometers from the confluence of the Iraqi, Syrian, and Turkish borders. On the western bank, then under the control of the Islamic State, was the farm where Zêdan grew up. Bacidkendala, the IDP camp where Jaff had lived, and Chammishkko, the IDP camp where Murad, his family, and Zêdan's still lived, were short drives away. In a landscape shaken by memories of violence, both recent and distant, the poets filled their nights with song, poetry, tears, and whiskey. Murad and Zêdan would often take long walks together during the day, outside the Chammishkko Camp, to forage for mushrooms, eat sunflower seeds, and sometimes, tracing the Kirkuk-Ceyhan Oil Pipeline until they arrived at a culvert, just to witness a stream of water. When Zêdan met Sahba and Sonita on the University of Duhok campus, the women joined them in reading clubs and on picnics.

A year later, invited by the Iraqi Writers Union to read in Baghdad, Saad joined the group. Bêrsivê, the IDP camp where he and his family lived, was east of Zakho, the city that separated Bêrsivê from Chammishkko. Still Zêdan and Saad met occasionally to smoke shisha, play backgammon or dominos, and, as always, talk poetry. Wacida, a musician and singer-songwriter as well as a poet, found Zêdan through a mutual friend, Fahad Herbo, who facilitated the introduction based on the shared desire they had to preserve Yazidi oral history, the songs and stories of traveling performers. Eventually mutual friends made online introductions to Shireen, based in the United States, and Janan, now in Germany.

The process of recovery is deceptively exhausting and complicated. When Zêdan sat for their collegiate entrance exams, they had nothing to wear but a tank top, capris, and shower sandals. Three weeks before that exam, they'd been separated from their family and fled to Shingal Mountain, eventually crossing on their own into Syria. Two weeks before the exam, they'd burned their feet crossing a metal bridge barefoot in scorching heat to re-enter Iraq. One week before the exam, on their nineteenth birthday, their family had escaped the village where the Islamic State had captured them. Two days before the exam, Zêdan had been reunited with their family. To arrive at the moment where the Student Housing Administration at the University of Duhok told them to post on Facebook for roommates, to meet Ameer, who got Zêdan to that apartment building where they eventually met Jaff; it is all so tenuous.

The poets, who kept reaching for themselves and for each other, even when they had no idea where they were as individuals or where their community was as a whole, have made this anthology real. This reaching is something Yazidi poets, singers, and storytellers have too much experience with. A Kurmanji-speaking minority indigenous to the Kurdistan region of Western Asia, which includes parts of the present-day states of Iraq, Syria, Turkey, and

Iran, Yazidis have distinct cultural and religious practices. Often labeled heretics by Islamic clerics and scholars, Yazidis have faced ongoing persecution since the early spread of Islam in the seventh and eighth centuries. Yazidism is an ancient, monotheistic ethnic religion. Religious Yazidis believe that God created the earth and entrusted its care into the hands of seven divine beings, including their leader Tawûsi Malek, the peacock angel, who holds authority over the earth. In fact, it is their reverence of Tawûsi Malek that is often cited as proof of their worship of Lucifer or Sheitan and used as a justification for their persecution.

Between 637 and 2014 CE, the Yazidis survived seventy-three attempted exterminations, primarily at the hands of surrounding Muslims, including the Safavids, Ottomans, and other tribes and principalities, both Arab and Kurdish. In the Yazidi oral tradition, which documents these persecutions and memorializes their victims, these extermination attempts are known as "farman," the Ottoman Turkish word meaning "decree," as such formal orders typically preceded what we today call genocide. These songs, performed in living rooms and backyards, in wedding halls and holy places, reached Emad and his family in exile in Syria on bootleg tapes and found Zêdan through pirate radio stations in Iraq. They recount the sacking of the holy city of Lalish, in 1254 and 1415, and the slaughter, in 1832, of seventy thousand Yazidis by Sunni Kurdish princes Bedir Khan Beg and Muhammad Pasha of Rawanduz. The latter, known in Yazidi stories as "the blind prince," fashioned a hill from the skulls of the Yazidis his army killed that he then climbed to preach from its peak, reciting Surah Al-Fath. The songs recount the deaths of an estimated three hundred thousand Yazidis indiscriminately murdered during the Armenian Genocide in 1915–16 and the British Army's attacks on Yazidi villages in the 1920s and '30s. More recent compositions recount the April 2007 massacre of twenty-three Yazidis kidnapped from a bus in Mosul and the August 2007 Qahtaniyah Bombings, when four coordinated suicide car bombs exploded in the Yazidi towns of Til Ezer and Sîba Sheikh Khidir, killing 796 and wounding over fifteen hundred more.

According to a 2016 report by the NGO Yazda, citing the UN Inquiry on

Syria, there were "no free [Yazidis remaining] in the Sinjar[1] region," where all these poets come from. The UN Inquiry goes on to say, "the 400,000-strong community had all been displaced, captured, or killed." Among those who had escaped capture or death, everyone had family members to find. Many of the elderly went into extended shock, unable to speak or truly live with the shame and powerlessness of watching videos widely circulated on TV and the internet of their children and women sold at the Islamic State's slavery market. The camps for internally displaced people were certainly not conducive to creating, rehearsing, gathering, or performing. The nylon tents of the camp prevented any kind of privacy. Zêdan's neighbors reported their eight-year-old brother to the police for playing tanbur and singing at the neighborhood children's bedtime. COVID-19 only worsened the state of Yazidi culture and cultural preservation. The elderly who were among those most susceptible to the virus were also the anchors of the vast lineage of Yazidi singers and storytellers.

There are no official statistics on how COVID-19 affected the Yazidi population, but current estimates tell us that ninety thousand Yazidis have migrated away from their ancestral lands and over three hundred thousand remain in IDP camps within the KRI, unable to resume life throughout Shingal. Even though the Islamic State did not entirely succeed in exterminating the population, the violence they unleashed did disperse the Yazidi people, disrupting, yet again, the modes of memory, creation, and healing Yazidis have turned to for centuries. Amid the displacement, the migration, and the inability to return to rhythms of normal life and gathering, traditional modes of song and storytelling have begun to disappear.

This recent trend compounded longstanding challenges first posed by Saddam Hussein's Baathist, Arabist Iraq and the policies of forced relocation of Yazidis from their mountain villages to more concentrated settlements starting in the 1960s and '70s. In these collective settlements, language

---

1. Sinjar is the Anglicized version of Shingal's Arabic name and is often used interchangeably with that spelling. In this anthology, we have prioritized the Anglicized Kurmanji place names.

illiteracy programs, forcing Arabic and banning Kurmanji, created an unprecedented generational gap in the community. Globalization and its technological byproducts, already present under Saddam and flooding the market in the wake of the U.S. Invasion of Iraq in 2003, facilitated and deepened this gap. Yazidi people of the generation of this anthology were displaced not only to new locations, but also to online worlds, meeting at cafes that offered free Wi-Fi with the purchase of shisha. Global soccer, global porn, global gaming, and global terrorism went a long way to drowning out traditional Yazidi stories and songs, to sweeping away the people who performed them and the people who listened.

Throughout history, the Yazidi people turned to epic poems to create, remember, and share their history, to celebrate their ecosystem and the gifts of their land, mountains, and waters. "May God never trouble any people, not even trees and plants, with the campaigns of a state," whispers one Yazidi epic that recounts the genocidal campaign led by Ibrahim Pasha, an Ottoman military general, referencing the scorched earth military tactic the Ottomans deployed, inflicting genocide not only on the targeted Yazidis, but on all living organisms. The poets of this anthology grew up listening to these songs in their households and at gatherings. Over the course of their lifetimes, they saw these poems struggle—and largely fail—to compete with TV and the internet for their attention. The epic stories and songs of the Yazidi oral tradition only reliably won out for attention during the frequent state-supplied power outages.

One form of healing that brought the poets of this anthology together was the return to their own community's modes of storytelling. Almost all of the poets included in this anthology are also singers, songwriters, musicians, preservationists, archivists, and translators. Editors Alana and Zêdan have worked alongside Emad and Wacida to preserve the endangered Yazidi oral traditions through Shingal Lives, an initiative co-led by Kashkul, the Center for Arts and Culture at the American University of Iraq, Sulaimani (AUIS) and Professor Christine Robins at the University of Exeter's Institute for Arab and Islamic Studies. Directed by Emad and Zêdan, the project has recorded 130 hours of interviews with eighty-five Yazidi elders, employing a team of twelve Yazidi oral historians. The Shingal Lives team designed and created the Tew Tew Archive as well as the Tew Tew Festival, a bi-annual festival gathering Yazidi storytellers and singers in the holy valley of Lalish.

No epics yet exist to recount the 2014 genocide. This anthology is, for the contributing poets as well as for readers, a continuation of the songs and stories they grew up loving, a continuation of what they've managed to preserve and what has been lost to them. These poets keep that tradition alive. This book is a celebration of Yazidi memory in the face of the tyrannies of colonization, the state, and the market that force forgetfulness on the people they strip from their resources.

Though Alana had briefly met Zêdan at a workshop she led in Duhok in 2016, we four editors connected several years later, in the fall of 2018, when Bryar and Shook, a researcher and artist in residence, respectively, at Kashkul, planned and hosted a reading featuring emerging Yazidi poets, including Zêdan, Emad, Jaff, Sarmad, and Saad. Preparation for that multilingual reading included translating some of the poems to be read, several of which now appear in more polished form in this anthology. Over the course of the busy years that followed, Zêdan and later Emad came to work for Kashkul, Bryar and Shook translated Zêdan's first book, and both Bryar and Zêdan left the region for graduate school—and all the while the idea for this anthology germinated, evolving into its present form that focuses on the poets most materially impacted by the events of August 2014. These poets write in multiple languages: their native Kurmanji, the medium of the Yazidi oral tradition as well as a robust twentieth century written literature; Arabic, the language of formal education in Iraq (which oversees the education system in Shingal today) and the Baathist Party's medium of forced cultural Arabization over the course of five decades; and even English, spoken in the places some have resettled or traveled to pursue their educations. The poets' dispersion reflects the broader Yazidi community's, another ongoing effect of the genocide. Of the eleven poets included, only two have returned to Shingal. Five live within the borders of the Kurdistan Region of Iraq, two live in Germany, two in the United States, and one in Greece.

It is our hope that this anthology, whose title comes from Zêdan Xelef's poem set at the kindergarten in the Chammishkko IDP Camp, join the songs recounting the seventy-three preceding farmans as the next chapter in an ancient testament to Yazidi suffering and survival, resilience and triumph, as well as standing as a condemnation of genocide and persecution on ethnic or religious grounds and a celebration of the shared humanity of all Yazidis and the talents of Yazidi poets and storytellers in particular. May their voices never become missing from this world.

The Editors
Newt Beach, California
January 2024

Emad Bashar

is a poet, scholar, digital archivist, and community organizer. He was born in Syria in 1992 to a Yazidi family from Shingal, where he returned after the U.S. occupation of Iraq and resided until the Islamic State's invasion. He is the author of three books of poetry, *Shadow* (2017), *You and I Look Alike* (2019), and *How the Fish Imagines the Wilderness* (2023). He currently lives in the village of Shariya in the Kurdistan Region of Iraq with his wife and their twins.

جثث الصبار المزرق

بشفاه مزرقّة
و شوكةٍ في حلقه
يشير المغني
إلى الكأس الفارغة
مبحوحاً
ينسى الأغنية
و يتوق
لخلاص أصابعه
التي
تغرق في وتر البزق الشائك

Bruised Cactus Corpses

With bluish lips
And a thorn lodged in his throat
The singer points
To the empty cup
His voice hoarse
He forgets the song
And yearns
To save his fingers
Drowning in the tanbur's thorny strings

'

البقعة الحمراء

أحلمُ دوما بفضائيٍّ مجنون
يرقص على حافة المشتري
يسترسل في الصراخ
متناغماً
مع ايقاع بقعةٍ حمراء كبيرة
في قلبي

صباحاً
اسمع صوت أقدامٍ حافية
تمشي على كتف جبلٍ ما
في قلبي

The Red Stain

I always dream of an insane alien
Dancing at the edge of Jupiter
And continuously transmitting screams
Synchronized with the rhythm of a big red stain
In my heart

In the morning
I hear the sound of bare feet walking
Treading on a mountain's shoulder
In my heart

البريّة في مُخيِّلة السمكة

الي: ناديا

صباحاً
و انت تحمل وحدتك
و تَمضي
يتضاءل النور القرمزي
للسرطان

*

من عدائية الواقع
تنبلج النظرة الأولى للحياة
منغمسةً في الشعاع
و كأن شيئاً ما يحملك
الي داخلٍ آخر
غرفةً في حزن غيرك
يتساءل الظلام!
عن سوداوية تلك الرغبة
في أن تكون الوحدة ملاذا

*

رمبا
على كلٍ منّا
جمع شظايا موتِه . . . مُتفائلاً

How the Fish Imagines the Wilderness

for Nadia

In the morning
When you carry your loneliness
And leave
The cancer's crimson light
Fades away

*

The first look at life dawns
From hostile reality
Immersed in the ray
As if something is holding you
To another body
To a room in someone else's sadness
Even darkness wonders
About the darkness of that desire
For loneliness to be a refuge!

*

Maybe
Each one of us
Must collect the fragments of our death . . . optimistically

قَمَر

الي: زيدان

لقد رصد الله لؤلؤةً في العدم
شيئاً وحيداً جداً
ليس من خلقه
عبثاً مضيئاً
فتساءل

Moon

for Zêdan

God spotted a pearl in the void
Something very lonely
Not of his creation
A luminous absurdist
And He wondered

(خليّة)

العشب
سجائر الأرض
الهواء : دخان نقي

التعلّق
غيومٌ جافة
التعلّق
خرقة عديمة الرائحة
التعلّق
عندما يتكرر الحب يصبح رماداً
و القصائد أيضاً ازهار
من غير طلع و لا تويجات
أوراق باهتة اللون
معلقة بساق الوجود

هنا حياة
أيتها النحلة السكرانة

هناك موت
أيتها القهوة الباردة

لفّ لي سيجارة يا جدي
حنجرتي ممتلئة بالدبابير

(cell)

The leaves of grass
Are the Earth's cigarettes
The air: pure smoke

Attachment
Is parched clouds
Attachment
Is a scentless rag
Attachment
Is when love repeats itself into ash
Poems into flowers
With no pollen no petals
Only pale leaves
Perched on the leg of existence

Here is life
Oh drunk bee

There is death
Oh cold coffee

Hey grandpa, roll me a cigarette
My throat is full of wasps

الغرق

قُمْ و أقِمْ للمدينة مأتماً
فالراحلون عن المدينة ميّتون
وأفرِغ قناديل القُرى

أسلك طريق البحر إن شئت
لكن لا تسأل الأمواج
ماذا جرى؟

فالبحر كان قبل الأمس عيناً
حجبتها جفون اليبسِ
فصارت لا ترى

والشمس نازحةٌ أخفاها المخيم
في دمعةٍ ثكلى
ففاضت أنهُرَ

كم من غريقٍ تحتاجهُ الأبدية
كي تحوّل النهر لوادٍ
يا تُرى؟

Drowning

Rise and hold a funeral for the city
Those who left the city are dead
Snuff out the village lamps

Take the sea route, if you will
But do not ask the waves
What happened

Until yesterday, the sea was an eye
Eclipsed by eyelids of land
And it became sightless

And the camp displaced the sun
Hid it in a heavy tear
That made the rivers flow

How many of the drowned does eternity need
To turn that river into a valley,
I wonder?

حصان الشطرنج يعدو نحو اغاني السكارى قرب النهر الذي جف من تعذر الدماء في المدينة، العود الذي قطع الجنود أوتاره تحول إلى طبل يدق عليه المشردون ، النبع التي كانت صبايا القرية تذهبن اليها كل صباح تحولت إلى ثدي كبير يرضع اطفال الغزاة ، الشجرة الباسقة في باحة منزلنا القديم أصبحت حبلاً لنشر بزات الضباط ، الأغنية التي سمعتها في طفولتي صارت غازاً مسيلاً للدموع ، الصديق الذي سافر قبل سنة من غير أن يودعني سمعت أنه أصبح بحيرة صغيرة في البلاد الغريبة ، وانا الذي كنت أحاول كتابة كل هذا اراني اتحول ببطء إلى قبلة واختفي في جبين جدتي.

The knight lopes across the chessboard towards the drunks' songs, past the river that dried up with the city's rising blood, and the oud whose strings the soldiers cut has been turned into a drum pounded by the displaced. The natural spring that the village girls used to visit each morning has become a swollen breast suckling the children of the invader, the plump tree in the courtyard of our house became a clothesline for the officers' fatigues. The song I heard in childhood became tear gas, the friend who left a year ago with no goodbye. I heard he became a small lake in a strange country, and I, trying to write all this down, see myself slowly transforming into a kiss that disappears on my grandmother's forehead.

العبيدُ

فتاتُ خبزٍ في الحظيرة
دمٌ
على الأسفلتِ
يغلي في شرايين الوجود
على حجر الحياة
يتمددون ليلاً
مهملين خرافة العمر القديم
الأغنياتُ وجعٌ
هم وترُ النشيد
وبقيّةُ اللحن الغريب
العبيد:
طريقة الصوت
وشجو الصامتين

ليتني عبدٌ
يقول بائع الكبريت
ويشعل آخر سيجارة

ليتني عبدٌ
يقول السائح التائه
ويرمي التأشيرة في البحر

ليتني عبدةٌ
تقول الفتاة الحليقة
وترتدي سترة المشفى

ليتنا عبيدٌ
يقول الباعة المتجولون
ويفترقون عند مشارف القرية

The Slave

A girl in the barn
Blood
On the asphalt
Boiling in the arteries of survival
They stretch out at night
On life's rocks
Ignoring the ancient myth
Their songs are pain
They are the string that voices the anthem
And the rest of the strange melody
The slave:
Both the mood of the sound
And the sorrow of the silent

I wish I were a slave
Says the match man
Lighting his last cigarette

I wish I were a slave
Says a lost tourist
Tossing his passport in the sea

I wish I were a slave
Says a girl with no hair
In a hospital gown

We wish we were slaves
Say the street vendors
Scattering at the outskirts of the village

ليتنا عبيدٌ

يقول السكارى فجراً

ويترنحون عائدين إلى الحياة

ليتني حرٌّ

يقول العبدُ وهو يرمي السلاسل

يقطع الطوق

ويعدو بفزع

يتعثر بالسكارى والباعة المتجولين

يصطدم بالفتاة الحليقة في الشارع

ويعدو بفزع

يصطدم بالسائح التائه وبائع الكبريت

يتوقف تحت شجرة زيزفون

عند قبرٍ

قرب كهفٍ

فوق تلّةٍ

بين القرية والمخيم والمدينة

ويغني:

" ارفعي الكأس ايتها الحياة

وانا سأسقط

كلا

اسقطي الكأس أيتها الحياة

وانا سأرتفع "

We wish were slaves
Say the drunks at dawn
Staggering their way back to life

I wish I were free
The slave says, casting off his chains
Snapping off his collar
Galloping in fear
He stumbles past the drunks and the vendors
He collides with the girl with no hair
Galloping in fear
He collides with the lost tourist and the match man
Pauses beneath the lime tree
At a grave
Near a cavern
On a hill
Between the village and the camp and the city
And sings:
Raise your cup, oh, life,
And I will fall,
No . . .
Drop your cup, oh, life,
And I will rise

Janan Dakhil

is a poet native to the Shingal mountains. She was forced to leave her home in the wake of the 2014 Yazidi genocide. She relocated to an unfinished concrete building in Zakho, in the Kurdistan Region of Iraq. Eight months later she moved to the Mamiliyan IDP Camp in Akra, where infighting between Yazidis and Muslims forced her to again relocate, this time to the Kabarto IDP Camp in Zakho. In 2017, she migrated to Germany, where she currently lives.

في وطني فقط
نار الحرب لا تخشى المطر
دموع الأمهات كفيلة بذلك

Only in my homeland
Do the fires of war not fear the rain
A mother's tears are enough

ذكي
من سرق كل فساتين القصيدة
سوى حزنها

Clever
The one who stole the poem's every dress
But its sadness

كيف لي؟

كيف لي ان أحبك في هذا العمر!
وانا وليدة من واقع ٤٧ ضحكة شائكة
أخشى عليك من شآبيب الهواء

*

مغرورة هذه الحرب
مذ ان قال لي ضحكتكِ جميلة
و هي لم تتوقف من دغدغة بكائي

*

لو الحرب
تأخرت لحظةً اخرى
لِ احببتك حباً كاملاً

*

انا لا يوجعني شيء
يوجعني قلبي
الذي مَلك الحب بوجه الحرب
و يعجز عن إفصاحُهُ!

How Can I?

How can I love you during these times!
And I am born from the reality of 74 thorny laughs
Even the breeze provokes my worry for you

*

Ah this arrogant war
Ever since it told me my smile is beautiful
It hasn't stopped tickling my tears

*

If the war
Had come just one moment later
I would have loved you fully

*

Nothing hurts
Except my heart
Pulsing with love in the face of war
With no explanation!

تركوا العشاق
واجعلوا من خدي ساحة حرب لكم
لتقتلوا بعضكم جُميعاً
فجمال خدي لا يهم
سوف أعتبر آثار المدافع غمّازات لي
وأعود كي أحب من جديد.

*

ما كان علينا أن نعوّل على الحب كثيراً
كي لا نموت في كل حربٍ تأتي

*

في بلادي
وحدها الخيمة تعرف
كم هي الجدران بائسة
بدون ظهر يستند إليها
حزني أكبرُ من خيمة
أنا للشتاء
والكلّ يسكنني

*

بالأمس
عندما ودّعتني أمي
عرفتُ من دموعها
كيف أنعشُ العمر من
نزيف الإبادات

Leave the lovers alone
And make my cheeks a battlefield
Where you all can kill each other
Their beauty is insignificant
I will embrace your artillery craters as dimples
And love you again

*

We shouldn't have relied so much on love
So we wouldn't have to die in every war to come

*

In my homeland
Only the tent witnesses
How miserable the walls are
With nothing to lean on
My sorrow outgrows my tent
I belong to winter
And boredom finds its dwelling within me

*

Yesterday
When my mother said goodbye
I knew from her tears
How to revive my life
Bleeding exterminations

لم يخبرونني
أنه لا يحق للقرويات أن يكتبن الشعر
الآن يا أمي
كيف اخيط ثوب القصيدة
و اغتالوا أناملي من تقاليدهم
جرفوا أحلامي كالقشة لآخر النهر

They did not tell me

That village women have no right to write poetry

Now, Mom

How to sew the dress of my poem?

They have assassinated my fingertips with their traditions

They swept my dreams to the mouth of the river, like a stalk of straw

Sahba Dexîl

is a poet and physics teacher. She received her B.A. in physics from the University of Duhok in 2018. Her work has previously been translated into Kurmanji. She currently lives in Shariya, in the Kurdistan Region of Iraq, where she relocated with her family in the wake of the Yazidi genocide in 2014.

ببطء أحاول
أجمعك، بكامل التفاصيل في قلبي
الابتسامة، شمس تطل من النافذة
الملامح، حقل الشيخوخة
رائحة التبغ
عيناك حيث اتجاه الروح
شعرك المكثف بالغيوم
الرصاصي في قميصك
ألتمس في الهواء دفء يداك

اعيد توازن
الحياة في جسدي
وأنا أشير إليك
أجد طفولتي الضائعة

اجمع كل التفاصيل التي تمكنني أن احيا
وأنا أخلقك!

أنك هنا الآن
لا أريد لأي شيء أن يشوه هذه الصورة
سأعلقها حول عنق الأبدية
الزمن ما بين قدماي والكرسي
أنه يمضي بسرعة
فجأة يتوقف

ثم هناك حركة
صوت الكرسي وهو يقع
أننا معا الآن
أمضي خطوة
لأقترب من الحياة التي صنعتها
اقترب
احاول ان المسها
يتناثر كل شيء
فراغ، فراغ أبدي

Gently, I try
To collect you, through every detail in my heart
Your smile, some sun peeking through a window
Your face, a senescent field
The scent of tobacco
Your eyes, the compass of my soul
Your hair, a thick cloud
The gray of your shirt
I feel the warmth of your hands in the air

I restore the balance
Of life in my body
I point to you
I find my lost childhood

I collect all the details that call me to life
And I create you

You are here now
I will keep your portrait pristine
I will hang it around eternity's neck
Between my feet and the chair, time
Bolts by
Then halts

Disturbance follows
The sound of the chair as it falls
We fuse
As I take one step further
To get closer to the life I created
Lean in
I extend my hand for a touch
This body disintegrates
Into void, eternal void

كان يقف على حافة النهر
صاح به النهر
ابتسم للنهر ثم اختفى

He stood by the edge of the river
The river shouted at him
He smiled at the river then disappeared

ساعة يدي توقفت عن النبض

هل هي عاطلة

أم انك هاجرت؟

My watch stopped ticking
Did she break
Or did you leave the country?

في منزلنا ساعة كبيرة، جميلة
من صنع الصين
وضعنا عليها قطعة قماش من الطراز القديم
ثم
بجانب حديقة المنزل
رسمنا دائرة
ووضعنا حجرا في المركز
كعقرب يمشي ظله مع حركة الشمس
لنعرف الأمكنة التي تتلاشى
بين الجهات
ولنميز بيننا وبين الريح

Our home boasts a big, beautiful clock
Made in China
We drape it in old-fashioned cloth
Then
Draw a circle
In our backyard
We mark the center with a stone
A shadow scorpion shifting with the sun
To map destinations disappearing
At the periphery
To tell ourselves apart from the wind

Murad Elo

is a poet and educator. He was born in Shingal in 1964. He earned his B.A. in administration and economics at the University of Mosul in 1994. He's a member of the Iraqi Writers Union and a writer for the Arabic-language website Al-Hiwar Al-Mutamaddin. He and his family were displaced to Chammishkko Camp by the genocide, and their house was looted by members of the Islamic State in the wake of their invasion. He is the author of numerous books of poetry: *My Old Friend* (Yazda, 2016), *A Clay Life* (Piramerd Printing House, 2016), *Hope on the Way: Spiritual Fragments and Letters* (Lina Publishing, 2020), and numerous books of prose, including *A Man from the North: Short Stories* (Culture Printing House, 2013), *Sîno: A Novel* (Daraweesh Publishing, 2019), and *The Shadowwalker: 74 Tales* (Jan Publishing, 2022). He currently lives with his family in Varden, Germany.

وصل ٱلْفُتور، وٱلْجَزع سُوَيْدَاء قَلبِك، قَبْل أن تَقطع نِصْف ٱلطريق؛ وشعرتْ بِٱلْإرهاق والتَّعب عِنْدمَا بدَا لَك

الدَّرْب طويلا.

العنْكَبة تبنِّي بيْتهَا، ويتداعى البيْتُ مِرارًا قَبْل أن تُكْمِل بِناؤه.

دائمًا، وَكَأنهَا المرَّة ٱلأُولى تَبدَأ العناكب البِنَاء مِن جديد.

أَلَّا يكْفيك ذِكْر ٱسْم صَديقنا؛ لِتبْدأ ثَانية عِندمَا تُتْعب؟

إن ذكَرْتُ ٱسْمه، يَزُول ظمأ قَلبِي، وينْتَشر فِي المكَان أريج محبَّته، وٱسْتَمرَّ في مسيرَتي رَغْم المشقَّات!

62

Not even halfway down the road and you're worn out, indifference and
   dread have taken root in your heart's marrow, you're downright exhaust-
   ed by the path that seems to stretch endlessly before you.
The spider builds her home, which collapses over and over even as she builds.
And still, she approaches reconstruction as if for the first time.
Isn't it enough? The mention of our friend's name? To urge the weary on
   once more?
I mention His name and quench my heart's thirst, scatter the scent of His
   love into every room, and hearten myself for what lies ahead, calamity
   included.

أهانوني كثيرًا يَا مَلاكِي، وليشعروني بِالْمزيد مِن الإهانة في مَمْلكتك اِستَوْلوْا على بَيتي وَقَريتي ووضعوني في خَيمَة فَارغة.

أنت أيضا عاقبتني، أرسَلت مطرًا مِدرارًا لِثلاثة أيَّام مُتتالية تَجلَّد بِهَا جُوع أطفالي. وَمِن خِلَال دُموعي الشَّبِيهة

بِمطرك أهْتُديت لِأمر مهم، وَقلَّت لِعائلتي الصَّغيرة:

"إنَّما هَذه مَشِيئَة صَديقِي!"

رَغْم اَلغُربة والبَرْد والجوع والانْكسار والشَّوْق، أرْسلْنَا لَك اِبْتساماتنَا الصَّامتة؛ فَكَان الرّضى ضيْفنَا اَلمُميز في تِلْك اللَّيالي!

They humiliated me, oh, my angel, in abundance and as if that weren't
    enough, within your kingdom, they seized my home, razed my village,
    and confined me to an empty tent.

You also punished me, for three consecutive days, you sent torrential rain
    that slaked
my children's thirst. My tears, kin to your rain, led me
toward an urgent thought, and I said to my little family,
"This is the will of my friend!"
Exiled, cold, starving, broken, longing, we lifted up our silent joy; each
    night, we hosted contentment, our peculiar guest!

الصامت

في عالم الأطفال، جميع الحيوانات تتكلم، وفي نصوص الشعراء، الطيور تغني، والزهور ترقص، وفي قصص الحبّ، الأشجار تسجّل مواعيد الغرام، وفي الكتب المقدسة الحشرات تبتهل.

في الطبيعة، المخلوقات من الفصيلة الواحدة تناغي بعضها.

الجميع يتحدثون؛ ليتعلم الإنسان منهم، والإنسان أخرس صامت.

The Mute

In the universe of children, every brute speaks, in the passages of poets,
    flowers
choreograph dances to birdsong, in tales on love,
Even old stumps record passionate trysts, and in the sacred books, insects
    lift their wings in prayer.
Throughout the natural world, even creatures of the same species chitter
    chatter.
Everything sings out in discourse; let man, dumb, mute man, learn.

طنبور الخلود

هربنا؛ لنبتعد عن أحزاننا، وعن الفرمانات التي تلاحقنا، وعند وصولنا إلى شاطئ الأمان رأينا طنبور طاف مقطوع الأوتار يتزاحم عليه أوجاع المهاجرين الغرقى.

شكرا حبيبتي،

شكرا؛ لأنكِ انتشلتني لحنا منسيا على أوتاره المقطوعة.

أقمنا على الشاطئ، أنا وأنت، وبنينا لنا بيتا على الرمال؛ وتكاثرنا، وأصبح عددنا أكثر من أوجاعنا التي تتزاحم على ذلك الطنبور الأخرس.

تعلمنا كيف نحزن، ونبكي مع أوتاره كلما غرق مهاجر.

كلما صرخ البحر.

كلما أهتز بيتنا المبني على الرمل.

The Tanbur of the Immortal

We ran away, fleeing our sorrows and the farman that haunt us. And when
we reached the safe shore, we saw a floating tanbur with its strings cut,
crowded with the pain of drowned migrants.

Thank you, my beloved,

Thank you, for pulling me a forgotten melody from its plucked strings.

We stayed on the beach, you and I, and we built our house on the sand. We
multiplied until we outnumbered our pains crowding that mute tanbur.

We learned how to grieve, how to cry with its strings every time a migrant
drowns.

Every time the sea screams.

Every time our house built on sand trembles.

Shireen Hasan

grew up in Til Ezer, a village on the south side of Shingal Mountain, until 2010, when her family moved to the United States because her father's work as an interpreter for the U.S. Army made remaining in their homeland unsafe. Today she is an English major at the University of Houston, and her writing connects her to her Yazidi roots.

She

She had her own beginning,
Paged out the empty land
We walk on.
She was the roof over our heads.
She was the ground under our feet.
She was the wall we leaned on.
She gave us a beginning full of
laughter, that we wrote across the walls.
Laughter that now echoes with pain.
Her chaos brought us safety and comfort
behind closed doors.
"Be safe," she cried,
as we would run across the concrete for sport,
as we fell over the cracks made by water.
She was our home while we were home.
Now she is a stranger.
Her cries bring us to our knees.
She continues to cry in agony.
We cannot save her.
She is left in a place she cannot leave.
Not all of her babies made it.
"Come my children! Come home!"
She cries when the sun goes to sleep.
"Where are you, loves!"
She cries when the sun awakes.
We yearn for her smell,
but fear has taken our minds.
She is all alone beside many others.
She is an anthem in memory,
waiting for the day her soul becomes a home.

August

You know those big hills
wept wet sand on August.
Rolls and rolls of sand on August.
Would they call August a friend or an enemy?
Was August the target or deadline?
The hills were red as far as the eye could see.
They sang a quiet sad muse
as salty, wet sand washed them out.
August,
August, our summer friend.
This was quite a winter.
Now you have become a stranger on the other side,
and who is to apologize now?
A vast one, just another.
Same smoke, bigger fire.
Same wounds, deeper burns.
Same roads closed by black armor.
Broken roads hid danger.
Loud fear flooded streets
Slowly possessing every soul.
Take what you hold dear
and go.
This one has come to haunt.
This one took practice.
You were watched,
you were played,
the same ones who gave you the seventy-third
dreamt of the seventy-fourth.
It was to be the end,
but it marked a greater beginning.

Lenny

Lineage gray and rusty
Smelling of everything I stray away from
It seems to grow by day
Everyone looks the same
They act the same
All scared and better than me
What did I ask for anyways?
Not this for sure
Not to be thrown out
Not to be played with
Not to have rocks thrown at me
Afraid of my own breathing
I don't want it
None of it
There is one door I find open and run inside
I seek shade because this heat kills me
I seek a couple of hours before the owners kick me out
With shoes, a broom, screams of shoo
They come looking for me every time
Banging this door I run to
Claiming I am theirs
I am not
One of my legs hurts
I must have stepped on god knows what
And I will keep stepping on whatever it was because I do not know any
    better
Forgive me for not being perfect
I never asked for this place or any other one
I do not have that luxury

All I want is to be left alone,
There is not much left
Let it end with peace and not this fear . . .

Jaff

is a poet, essayist, translator, and psychologist. He was born in 1994 in the town of Sîba on the southwest side of Shingal Mountain. He is the translator into Kurmanji of Murad Elo's *My Old Friend* and Nawal El Saadawi's *The Fall of the Imam*, as well as dozens of poets to appear in the language for the first time. Today he lives in Shariya, in the Kurdistan Region of Iraq, and writes for Academia Post Society, an Arabic-language website. As a form of resistance against the forced Arabization that began with his grandfather's family's forced relocation in the 1970s, Jaff shortened his own Arabic birth name to its present form, "a meaningless name chosen for its simplicity, ease of forgetting, and insignificance."

Delirium

Li ber derê vê xîvetê me
Di navbera min û kolanê de
Heft gav
Zarokê ku ev bîst û çar salan mirî
Kevirên xwe tavêje pencerê
Û direve
Ew keça min jê hezkirî
Heft nameyan li dora min bizar dike
Û wenda dibe
Hevalê min yê nebûyî
Behsa teşqeleyên xwe dike
û direve
Li destpêka rê
û li dawiya rê
Zarokek berev kalekî
Kalek berev zarokekî
Baz dide
Min jî dixwest bazbidim
Wenda bibim
Eger lingên min asê nebane
Li tevna demê de

Delirium

In front of the entrance to my tent
Between me and the street
Seven steps
The child who died twenty-four years ago
Throws his stones at the window
And runs away
The girl I loved
Sows seven epistles around me
And disappears
My nonexistent friend
Tells me his plights
And runs away
At the beginning of the path
And at the end of the path
They leap
A child towards an old man
An old man towards a child
I too long to leap
To disappear
If only my feet weren't caught
In the cobwebs of time.

Çîroka du xîvetan

Rojê sed carî
Hewil didim vî zarokî têbigehînim
Xweveşartina li pişt dergehan de
Çûna serban
Dîtina mirîşk û baranê li pencerê re
Cuhtek pêlvav
Tenê efsaneyek

The Story of Two Tents

Today and for the hundredth time
I tell this child:
Hiding behind doors
Climbing on the roof
Staring at the rain and the chickens through the window
Wearing a pair of shoes
Pure myth

مرج متحجر

ما يبدو المخيم عليه

ربّاتُ فنون الهلاك يقطفن منه

الوجوه المحتفظة بدهشتها البكر—

وجوه هشة أمام سماكة الستارة

الأجساد تتقافز عراة

لتصير هباء—

ثمرة الخلق المنتظرة

A petrified meadow

The camp appears to be

Goddesses of the arts of eternal damnation pluck from it

Faces preserving their original wonder—

Faces fragile against a luxurious curtain

Bodies leap naked

Turning to dust—

Creation's awaited fruit

أستعيد نفسي من الآخرين

كلحظة ناقصة من الولادة

كأبدية زائدة في العمر

أستعيد نفسي من الآخرين

في الصباح، أتركه يستريح

لعله تعب من الشرح

أحاول ألا أثير صفوه بسؤال

لا أحسبه ضيفا ولا شريكا في شؤون اللغة

بالكاد أتذكر ما قاله آخر مرة

للرد على أي التباس قد يقع بيني وبينه:

احرص على ألا أقول «أنا» بصوت مسموع أو في عبارة قد تخضع لتعددية المعنى

أو أعطي مقدمة توضيحية وامنح لكل منا علامة ولكي لا يعتبر ذلك تدخلا في حياته اكتفي بالقول: أعد

نفسي من الآخرين

أولئك الذين يتشاركون في حروب بلاد بعيدة ويفضلون الربيع والقهوة وموسيقى الجاز

ذات مرة، صدفة دخلنا المقهى ذاته فطلبتُ شايًا

ورغم أنني استعملت الإشارات اللازمة لم يفرقوا بيننا

فتركته وفي قلبي رغبة لا تقاوم في إيجاد أقصر طريق إلى المنزل

منذ سنوات، لا أرى فيه آثار الندم ولا رغبة في محادثة بسيطة:

يدخل الغرفة ويتصرف بحرية كاملة، يفتح التلفاز، يغير ملابسه أمامي، يدخن، يشرب ويغني

لا أعطي لنفسي حق الاعتراض لكنني تمنيت ولو أخبرته بأنني أخاف من النوم في العتمة

يعد عيد ميلادنا أزمة دورية

نجلس وجها لوجه

ولكل منا طريقته في استجواب الآخر

نحدق في بعضنا البعض

وكأننا نحفر حفرة لنصل إلى الطرف الآخر من العالم

I reclaim myself from others

Like a missing moment from birth

Like an excess of eternity in life

I reclaim myself from others

In the morning, I let him rest

Perhaps he's tired of explaining

I try not to disturb his serenity with a question

I don't consider him a guest or a partner in matters of language

I can barely remember what he said last time

To respond to any confusion that may arise between us:

I make sure not to say "I" aloud or in an ambiguous phrase

Or I provide an explanatory introduction and give each of us a symbol, so
    as not to be considered an intrusion into his life, I simply say: I reclaim
    myself from others

Those who take part in the wars of distant lands prefer spring, coffee, and
    jazz music

Once, by chance, we entered the same café, so I ordered tea

And despite using the necessary signals, they couldn't differentiate between us

So I left, with an irresistible desire in my heart to find the shortest way home.

For years, I have seen in him no sign of regret nor a desire for simple conver-
    sation:

He enters the room and behaves freely, turns on the TV, changes clothes in
    front of me, smokes, drinks, and sings

I don't grant myself the right to object, but I have wished I could tell him
    that I fear sleeping in the dark

Our birthdays are periodic crises

We sit face to face

And each of us has his way of questioning the other

We gaze at each other

As if we're digging a hole to the other side of the world

Sonita Khalil

is a poet and biology teacher. She was born on a farm in Girzerik on the north side of Shingal Mountain during a famine so severe that her mother told her, "The year you were born, we almost starved to death." She grew up in the village of Til Qeseb on the south side of the mountain, where she recalls her fellow children's joy at hearing the horn of the car that sold pomegranates. She was displaced with her family in 2014 in the wake of the Yazidi genocide and she has been forced to move many times since. She attended the University of Duhok, where she received her B.A. in biology in 2017. Her poems have previously appeared in numerous Arabic-language outlets including *Ultra Sawt* and *Alantologia*. She currently lives and writes in Germany, where she also works as an interpreter.

هل من أحد يجيد الحديث إلى الفراغات؟

يرفض أن يمتلئ؟

لماذا هناك واحداً منهم دائماً

وحده يرفض أن يمتزج بأي شيء

يعاندك حتى آخر نفس له

سّجان له ظهر مستقيم أملس

يراقب السجناء التعساء

يأتون ويرحلون

الهَم لهم يثبت على ظهره

يسجنك من الداخل

لا يبقي لك إلا ثقباً صغيراً

ترى من خلالهِ وهو يكسر،

إسطوانات الموسيقى المفضلة لديك

يغرس فيك صوت تحطمها

تحرق قصائدك الطوال

ويشعلها ناراً

تلك التي كانت تحتفظ لك بجمال الطرقات وروعة القمم

فراغ يُفَضل البقاء وحيداً منعزلاً

عزلته ظلام يغشي عينيك

يصم أذنيك

يسرق الحواس ويبقى فارغاً منها

فراغ يُشعر

جداره مصنوع من مجموعة كبيرة من الخيبات

سبّبه أناس تافهون

عقول متحجرة

قلوب جبانة

تناقضات كثيرة

النفاق

والانفس التي هربت منها البراءة

ولأنها أشياء لا مكان لها هنا في داخلك

تكُون فراغاً من بعيد

Is there anyone who can speak to the void?
Resist fullness?
Why is there always someone
Who alone resists blending with anything
Who supports you even with his last breath
A prison guard with a straight, smooth back
Watches the wretched prisoners
Come and go
Their burdens on his back
Who imprisons you from within
A small hole is all that's left you
You peer through as it fractures
Your favorite CDs
The music of their shattering sets a fire in you
That tears through your towering poems

And the one who sets the fire
The one who kept the beautiful roads and splendid peaks for you
Is a void who prefers sustained solitude, isolation
Whose oppressive isolation clouds your eyes
Who deafens you
Who steals your senses and is still empty
Feels empty
Whose wall is a considerable collection of disappointments
Petty people
Petrified minds
Cowardly hearts
Abundant contradictions
Hypocrisy
And the souls' innocence abandoned
Such things have no place here inside you
You become a distant void

وهي تضحك
مخلِّفةً جثة ترقص الوحدة على صدرها
وينهشها كغراب جائع

Laughter
A lonely corpse dancing on its chest
A crowbar
A hungry crow gnaws on

لا أحد هنا

وحدك تجالس بؤسك

وحدها وحدتك تعانقك

وحدك تحمل رأسك الثقيل

وحده ظهرك الذي يتقوس تحت وطأة آلامك

وحدك تعاني من التصاق ماضيك بجبينك

وحدك تراقص الخوف نحو تبهم مستقبلك

وحدك هنا

وحدك تشعر بدوارك

وحدك تسقط

هذا السقوط سقوطك وحدك

وهذا الصوت هو صوت ارتطامك بالأرض

ذاك النهوض القادم هو نهوضك

هذا العكاز يدك

هذا الشق هو طريقك

هذا المتناثر حوله هي أظافرك المنتزعة

هذا الذي يدغدغ وجهك هو عرقك

وحدك تراقب مشواره،

يبدأ من جبينك وينتهي على ذقنك

وحدها شفاهك تمتص ملح عينيك

وحدك تصل،

أو لن تصل

وحدك تبتسم أو لن تفعل

ادخل أولاً

ووحدك تقرر إذا كنت ستغلق الباب خلفك

أو تدعهم يدخلون

No one here
You alone sit with your misery
Your loneliness alone embraces you
You alone carry your heavy head
It's just your back that bows against the weight
You alone suffer your past stuck to your forehead
You alone dance in fear toward the uncertain
Here alone
You alone feel dizzy
You alone fall
This fall is yours alone
This sound is the sound of your body hitting the earth
The next rising is your body rising
This crutch is your hand
This crevice your road
Littered with torn fingernails
What tickles your face is your own sweat
You alone watch it stroll
From your forehead to the ledge of your chin
Only your lips sip the salt from your eyes
You arrive alone
Or you won't arrive at all
You smile alone or you won't
Go in first
You alone decide whether you close the door behind you
Or let them in

ضع رائحة طهي أمي
وركضي منتصف النهار
متعبة أرمي كتبي المدرسية
أحذيتي السوداء وأربطة ءُ شعري البيضا
ليمتلئ المكان بالفوضى
وتتبع فوضاي المنتشرة
من عتبة الباب وصولاً للمائدة
تراني أكلتُ كُل الطعام بأنفي وعيني
قبل أن أفتَح فمي

ضع توبيخ أخي الشديد
لأني نسيتُ أن أكوي قميصه

فلتتوقف، فلنضع الكثير في هذا التوقف
مشاركة ثياب إخوتي وشجاراتنا الكثيرة

دفءُ حضن أمي وضربُها المؤلم
قسوتُها الكثيرة وحبها الكبير
وجهها العابس ويدا أبي الفارغتان
صوتُها الكثير وصمتُ أبي الهائل

اغادر إلى عائلتي الاخرى
ألعابي
أيَن رحلوا؟
ألم أعش بينهم كثيّرا؟
كيف رميتهم؟ بعدَ أن كبرت؟
ولماذا؟

The scent of my mother's cooking rises
As I run in around noon
Tired, I toss my schoolbooks somewhere
My black shoes and my white hair ties
Filling the place with chaos
Letting my chaos sprawl
From the doorstep all the way to the table
I eat everything with my nose and eyes
Before I can even open my mouth

I listen to my brother's stern scolding
I forgot to iron his shirt

Let our watches stop ticking and our hearts measure time
Stealing my siblings' clothes and all our squabbles
My mother's tender embrace and severe beatings
Her ample cruelty and endless love
Her surly face and my father's empty hands
Her colossal voice and his abundant silence

I escape to my other family
My dolls in their house
But where did they go?
Should I have spent more time with them?
Did I grow out of them? Throw them away?
Why?

أحتاج لقفزات سريعة

كي لا يبتلعني الوحل

كي لا أعلق فيه

بعض من القفز السريع يُنقذ

كي لا أعلق في كلمة جارحة،

في أغنية حزينة،

أو في موقف بائس

أحتاجُ لقفزات سريعة

أن أقفز فوق الشيء

وكأني طفلة تلعب الحجلة

أن لا أعلق فيه

أن لا أمتص بؤسه

أحتاج أن ابتسم لأقفز

كي أنجو

كي لا يبتلعني الوحل

كي لا أعلق

I must jump quick
So the mud can't swallow me
I can't get stuck
A few quick jumps will salvage
An acrid word
A sorry song
Any miserable footing
I must jump quick
Over whatever
A child at hopscotch
I can't get stuck
I can't take misery in
I need to grin to jump
To live
The mud can't swallow me
I can't get stuck

Sarmad Saleem

is a poet, activist, and humanitarian from Xanesor. He is widely published in Arabic-language literary magazines and online outlets. His first book of poetry, *He Died Many Times, and There Was No Less Space in the Cemetery*, was published in 2022 by the Grand Library in London. He has participated in numerous poetry festivals across Iraq. He currently lives in the village of Shariya, in the Kurdistan Region of Iraq, with his family.

لم تكن لمنزلنا نوافذ
ولا أبواب
كنا نعيش في مربع صغير جدا
ترى كيف دخلت الحرب؟

Our house had no windows
And no doors
We lived inside a very small square
I wonder, how did the war get in?

قد تكون المدينة بخير

والبيوت صالحة للسكن ألف مرة أخرى

إنهم يتوقعون

إنهم يحلمون

إنهم يعودون

دون أجوبة لقليل أسئلتهم

دون رؤية غودو الذي انتظروه طويلا

حتى دون أي رغبة في الوصول

يعودون

Perhaps, their houses are a thousand times more habitable
They anticipate
They dream
They return
Their few questions remain unanswered
Still waiting on their promised Godot
Even with no desire to arrive
They still return

لسنوات

أمي كانت تعلمني الرجولة

حرفا حرفا

ثم جاءت أختي

اثر خطأ غير مقصود

كما يقول أبي

كبرت قليلا

وعندما أتقنت اللغة

لحسن حظي

أفسدت التعاليم كلها

هل تعرف ماذا ينقص رجولتك يا صديقي؟

تاء التأنيث

For years
My mother taught me manhood
Letter by letter
Then my sister was born
Following an accident
As my father would say
She grew up a little
And when she learned language
To my luck
She fucked the family teachings
You know what your manhood lacks?
Any sign of the feminine

مات الحطاب

مات الحطاب

قالت شجرة الرمان

ورقصت في باحة منزلنا

خرجت إلى الشارع

رأيت أرملة توزع الخبز على الفؤوس الصغيرة

The logger is dead
The logger is dead
Sang the pomegranate tree
As she danced in our front yard
I went out in the street
I saw a widow woman
Handing out bread to every little axe

البس كعب أمي

وأخرج إلى شوارع شنكال

أقول للأرض

عادت

عادت

عاد . . . وأسقط على وجهي

I put on my mother's high heels
And go out on the streets of Shingal
I tell the whole world
She's back
She's back
She's baa . . . and I fall flat on my face

الطفل الذي قطع الطريق من الجبل إلى روج آفا
بحذائه أكبر من مقاسه
وحده يعرف أسماء الجنود الذين تركوا أحذيتهم
في شنكال

Only the child who crossed the border
From Mount Shingal to Rojava
In too-big boots
Knows the names of those soldiers
Who left their boots behind

مرحبا

اسمي رنا.

عمري ثلاث عشرة سنة، ابنة شاعر يعاني من اضطراب الهوس الضاحك، نعيش معاً، وحيدين تقريباً، في منزل يضج برائحة الخمر وصوت فيروز ليلاً وعبد الباسط صباحاً، أبي يحبّ الحياة من طرف واحد منذ سنين طويلة والعزلة أيضاً.

اسمي رنا.

لم أدخل المدرسة، لأنّ أبي يعتقد بأنها مكان للنسيان والتعرف إلى أصدقاء السوء والمعلمين الفشلة ذوي البطون الكبيرة، هؤلاء الذين لا يعرفون كيف يفتحون النوافذ، يتحدثون كالببغاوات، ولا يتركون لنا فرصة لنقول لهم: أنتم على خطأ.

اسمي رنا.

الآن أعيش في قرية صغيرة، لنا جارة تدعى كامو، السيدة كامو امرأة ثلاثينية طلقت زوجها يوم ٢٠١٦/٠١/٠١ وراحت تربي كلباً أبيض، كلما شعرت بالحاجة إلى شيء ما جلبه لها من أحد منازل الجيران؛ مرة عندما كانت تشعر بالجوع ذهب إلى بيت أم حبيب وعاد بـ «طنجرة الدولمة». وعندما أرادت أن تتذكر عيد زواجها، عضّ الكلب أبي وهو في طريق العودة من الحانة، في الوقت الذي زار الشرطي السيدة كامو ليبلغها بضرورة الحضور إلى المخفر للتحقيق بسبب عدم دفعها فواتير الماء والكهرباء منذ ٤ سنوات، لم يستطع الوصول إلى باب منزلها، فاضطر أن يستخدم مكبر صوت (يبدو هذه الكلب شبيهي: أنا أيضاً أكره الشرطة).

أتذكر أيضاً.. أراد أحد سكان القرية قتل الكلب، حمل مسدساً وراح يبحث عنه؛ كم كان غبياً! كان الكلب يمشي خلفه ولم ينتبه؛ واستمرت الحال لعدة أشهر إلى أن سمعنا خبر انتحار رجل برصاصة في الرأس. نجح الكلب في أن يوفر كل شيء للسيدة كامو حين عجز أبي.

اسمي رنا.

أريد عندما أكبر أن أعيش في منزل ريفي مع كلب، الزواج قرار أحمق ومؤسسة فاشلة.

اسمي رنا.

أبي رجل لم يكن صالحاً للزواج، وكذلك للحياة.

Hi,

My name is Rana.

I am thirteen years old. My father is a bipolar poet. We live together in the same house, almost lonely, in a house buzzing with the smell of booze, the voice of Fairuz at night and Abdul Basit in the morning. My father is in an unrequited love affair with life and solitude for years now.

My name is Rana.

I did not start school, since my father believes it's a place for oblivion, meeting bad friends, and pot-bellied loser teachers who parrot on and on, don't know how to open windows, and don't allow us to tell them: YOU ARE WRONG.

My name is Rana.

I live in a small village now. We have a neighbor named Kamo. Mrs. Kamo is a thirty-year-old divorcee who broke up with her husband on 10/10/2016 and adopted a white dog. Whenever she needs anything, her dog hunts it down for her at a neighbor's house. Once, as her stomach growled, he snuck into Umm Habeeb's house and came back with a pot of dolma. When she wanted to reminisce about her anniversary, her dog bit my father on his way back from the inn. And when a policeman came to Mrs. Kamo's door to summon her to the police station, probing after the water and electricity bills that have gone unpaid for the past four years, her dog barked at him so he had to use his megaphone. Her dog seems like me—I hate the police too.

I also remember—a villager wanted to kill her dog. He grabbed his six-shooter and went out to look for him. What a fool he was! The dog dogged him but he did not notice him. He kept looking for the dog for months, until we heard about a man's suicide by a bullet to the head.

The dog succeeded at providing everything for Mrs. Kamo, while my father failed.

My name is Rana.

When I grow up, I want to live in a village house with a dog. Marriage is a foolish decision and a failed institution.

My name is Rana.

My father was not fit for marriage, nor for life.

ما وصلني الآن على البريد الإلكتروني من سركون بولص

عزيزي سرمد أنت وحيد

لا أصدقاء لك

تعيش في قرية مهجورة على ذكريات وصور لمن تحب

جميعهم رحلوا منهم إلى المنافي

ومنهم إلى المقابر الجماعية

أعرف هذا جيدا

صوتك لا يصل أبدا

مرة أردت أن أسمعك من بعد غير أن جان دمو وقف بيننا

كنت وقتها تحب إمرأة من بغداد تكره رائحة العرق والسجائر

عزيزي سرمد رجاءا لا تتحدث بعد الآن لا الأصدقاء لا الله لا أنا لا أحد منا يسمعك

I just received an email from Sargon Boulos

Dear Sarmad, you are all alone

No friends for you

You live in a deserted village, off the memories and photos of your loved ones

They've all fled

Some into exile

Others to mass graves

I know this very well

Your voice is never heard

Once I wanted to hear you from afar, but Jan Damo stood between us

At that time you were in love with a woman from Baghdad, a woman who
    hated the smell of arak and cigarettes

Dear Sarmad, please shut up, none of us—not your friends, not God, not
    me—hear you

Saad Shivan

is a poet, teacher, and IT technician. He was born in Xanesor, on the north side of Shingal Mountain. He has participated in literary festivals across Iraq and his work has appeared in numerous Arabic outlets, including *Al-Akhbar*, *Al-Arabi*, and *Iraqi Palm*. His debut collection *Tent 13* was published in 2023 by Noor Books. After the genocide, he lived in Bersivê Camp with his family. He currently resides with his wife as a refugee in Mykonos, Greece.

لدينا بيت من طابقين في شنكال وفناء صغير
أمي لا تذكر منه سوى تنور الطيني
الذي يقع خلفه
كل شيء قابل للنسيان
إلا الخبز هناك

We have a two-story house in Shingal with a small courtyard
My mother only recalls the clay oven
Nestled in our backyard
Everything is forgettable
Except the bread baked there

خلف السياج

عند دائرة تسجيل متطوعي

الشرطة

كان

واقفا بكل وساخته

قال للشرطي

أبي مات

بلغة عربية ركيكة

الحرب ت ربما قتله

الشرطي لم يفهم شيئا

طفل شنكالي

واصل البكاء

ما أوسخ

أن لا يعرف

الآخرون

معنى موت ابيك؟

Behind the fence
At the police
Volunteer recruitment center
A Shingali child
Standing in all his filth
Spoke to the policeman
In broken Arabic
My father died
The war must have taken him
The policeman failed to understand
The child
Continued crying
How filthy is it
That no one understands
The meaning of your father's death?

أمي تستلم ماكنة الخياطة من منظمة هاريكار بتاريخ ٥٠/٤٠/٢٠١٧

سوف ينشرون هذا

سيقولون إنك حية، وإن أطفالك يعيشون حياة جميلة ورائعة

وإن زوجك يرتدي بذلةً باهظة بربطة عنق حمراء وهو يخرج إلى العمل في الصباح

سيقولون إن ماكنةَ الخياطةِ جعلت حياتهم أفضل بكثير مما كانت، وإننا سعداء جدا

سيقولون اشياء كثيرة عنّا

حينما تكونين مشغولةً بوضع الإبرة في عيوننا لتجنب المزيد من الدموع في هذه الحرب

My mother receives a sewing machine from the Harikar NGO on
04/05/2017

They will post this
They will say that you are alive, and that your children are living a wonderful
life
And your husband wears an expensive suit with a red tie as he sets off for work
each morning
They will say that the sewing machine has made their life much better than it
was, and that we now brim with happiness
They will have so much to say about us
While you're caught up, piercing our eyes with needles to stop further tears in
this ongoing war

كأي أب شنكالي يبدو خشنا ومتعبا

في سيباي صادف عمره حروب لم يمت فيها

في ٢٠٠٧ انشقت البيوت إلى شقين والآن هي مفخخة بالديناميت وما شابه

*

ثمة أحداث لا يعيش الإنسان بعدها إلا ليكون

مثل نفخة في الهواء تتلاشى بأسرع وقت ممكن

ثمة طعنات قاتلة تستغرق العمر كي تستكمل عملها بشكل تام

أبوك مثل النهر؛ شرب دماء كثيرة،

لنفهم أنه الآن يعيش ايضا

هي الحياة تذوب بسرعة في الحروب

Like any Shingali father, he looks rough and tired
In Sîba, he survived a lifetime of wars
In 2007, the houses split in two and now they're rigged with dynamite and
    the like

    *

There are times a person does not live beyond, except just to exist
Like a puff of disappearing air
There are fatal stabs that take a lifetime to complete their work
Your father is like a river—he drank a lot of blood
To understand that he was still alive
Life so quickly dissolves into war

في قريتي القديمة اقصد قبل الحرب
اكرر القديمة
كنا نرافق التوابيت التي تخرج الى الشوارع
ملفوفة بالبطانية وليس علم البلد
حينها ايضا لم نكن نملك بلدا حقا على اقل لم
نشعر بذلك
كانوا يتحدثون عن المال الذي يمكن ان يجنيه
أحدهم من الحدود بتهريب السجائر والبنزين
وفي الصباح تعلن السماء المعتقلين والمصابين بالرصاص
لم نكن نخون أحدا أعني ذلك لم نملك بلدا
ذخائره الفارغة التي نجلبها من وراء التوابيت كانت
تتحول الى صافرة
كي ننبه العالم ان يشرح لنا
ما معنى الطفولة حقا في قرانا؟

In my old village, I mean before the war
I repeat, the old one
We accompanied the coffins marching through the streets
Wrapped in blankets, not the country's flag
We didn't really have a country then,
Or at least that's how we felt
They were talking about the money he could have earned
Smuggling cigarettes and gasoline across the border
In the morning, the sky announces the detained and shot
We were not betraying anyone—I mean, we had no country
We crafted whistles from
The spent shells we gathered in the coffins' wake
To remind the world to explain to us
In our villages, what does "child" really mean?

ما يطلق عليهم بالنازحين
هم بالأحرى الفراغات
التي يتركها القتلة
في كل حرب

What you call displaced people
Are rather the gaps
The killers in every war
Left behind

الساعة تشير الى ١:٠٠ صباحا

انا نازح سعد، على ما يبدو حياتي لا معنى لها في بلد الاسلام

انا من اقلية بائسة، تبحث عن هوية مثل منزل محترق

وانا ابن فاشل لأم مريضة وأب ميت

تحمل أمي عرق سنوات النزوح مثل حبل الغسيل رغم اصياف كثيرة لم يجف

أكره هذه الكوميدية المتواصلة

*

انا من اقلية بائسة، تدعى الايزيدية

لنا أعياد كثيرة

والمؤمن منا لا يغتسل في الاربعاء

لا آبار النفط في شنكال حيث كنا نسكن، ولكن أؤكد لكم

اننا اغنياء بالمقابر الجماعية

The clock shows 1:00 AM
I am displaced Saad, my life seemingly meaningless in the land of Islam
I come from a miserable minority, searching for my identity like a burnt-out
     house
I am the failed son of a sick mother and a dead father
My mother bears the sweat of years of displacement like a clothesline, and
     despite many
summers it has not dried
I hate this non-stop comedy

     *

I come from a miserable minority, called the Yazidis
We have many holidays
The believers among us do not bathe on Wednesday
There are no oil wells where we lived in Shingal, but I assure you
We are rich in mass graves

Zêdan Xelef

is a poet, translator, archivist, and culture preservationist. They were born on a farm near the confluence of the Tigris and Khabour rivers on the Iraq-Syria border, where they waved at the departing trains with the first light of the day. They grew up in the village of Izêr on the south side of Shingal mountain, where they herded four goats along with three of their cousins. They are the author of *A Barcode Scanner* (Kashkul Books, 2021/Gato Negro Ediciones, 2022), poems written in and about Chammishkko Camp, where they lived with their family for five years after being displaced from their village in the wake of the 2014 Yazidi genocide perpetrated by the Islamic State. The title poem of the book was adapted into a poetry film by Shook and received the Award for Best Film for Tolerance at the 2020 ZEBRA Poetry Film Festival in Berlin. Xelef's poetry and translations have appeared in numerous literary outlets, including the *Los Angeles Review of Books*, *World Literature Today*, *Poetry London*, *Tripwire*, *Conjunctions*, and *Poetry*. Their selection and translation of Selim Temo's poems, in collaboration with Alana Marie Levinson-LaBrosse, came out under the title *Nightlands* from Pinsapo Press in 2024. They currently live and write in Oakland, California.

قارئ باركود

قِطاعُ خِيَم فشارعُ زفت فقطاع خيم

في البدءِ كان الرقم والرقمُ صارَ سعراً والتصقَ بنا
وسهّل الرقم إنتقاءنا عن بعد دونما إستعانة بالسَبّابة
ثم صارتُ الأرضُ مذياعاً وببطارية أبدية لا يبثُّ محطةً ولا يكفُّ عن
التشويش

شارع زفت فقطاع خيم فشارع زفت

نُرُبّينا على كره الموت وحب الموت
نُرُبّينا على حب الحياة وكره الأحياء
يغني لا أحد المجنون وهو يهرب من مراهقين يحاولون نزع
بيجامته عنه

قطاع خيم فشارع زفت فقطاع خيم

النازحُ حمارٌ وحشي في عراء مسيّج
ويتصفّح منشورات مجموعة مغلقة على الفيسبوك

شارع زفت فقطاع خيم فشارع زفت

فلتبيضّ عيناك وتصير جثة الطاووس رقعة عين لك أيها القرصان التائه
دُعاء أمهات جائعات يطبخن الملل على أبناء يشخرون في منتصف النهار
في كل خيمة

قطاع خيم فشارع زفت فقطاع خيم

من يُعرِّفُ النازح بشروق الشمس؟
من يقنعه أن للشمس أي غرضٍ آخر غير بث الحرارة؟

شارع زفت فقطاع خيم فشارع زفت
الزوبعة التي تدخل الخيمة وتُطَيّرها عن رأسك ليست سوى رقصا صوفيا

A Barcode Scanner

Tent block, then muddy street, then tent block

In the beginning there was the number and the number became a price tag
    stuck to us
The number made our selection easier from afar, no need to point
Then the earth became a radio with an eternal battery, no broadcast station,
    and no stop to
  the disruption

Muddy street, then tent block, then muddy street

We raise ourselves on the hatred of death and the love of the dead
We raise ourselves on the love of life and the hatred of the living!
The crazy nobody is singing while teenagers chase him, trying to strip off his
    pajamas

Tent block, then muddy street, then tent block

The IDP is a zebra in a fenced-in wilderness
Browsing the statuses of a closed Facebook group

Muddy street, then tent block, then muddy street

May your eyes cloud over and the peacock's corpse become your eyepatch,
    deviant pirate
The prayer of hungry mothers, boiling boredom for their children, who
    snore through midday
  in every tent

Tent block, then muddy street, then tent block

Who introduces the IDPs to sunrise?
Who convinces them that the sun serves any purpose but heat?

للحياة الزاهدة الساخرة منك

قطاع خيم فشارع زفت فقطاع خيم

مادّاً يده وماسكًا البطاقة التموينية
هكذا يسير النازح في الشوارع بحثا
مثل مستشعر ألغام

شارع زفت فقطاع خيم فشارع زفت

بائع الطماطم ليته مهرجان التراشق بالطماطم يقام هنا لمرة واحد على
الأقل
لينعم الشعب برؤية الأحمر بطريقة أخرى

قطاع خيم فشارع زفت فقطاع خيم

بائع البصل: فلتحيا الحياة
بائع الباذنجان: هاهاهاها

قطاع خيم فشارع زفت فقطاع خيم

الحياة في المخيم ياسٌ مُشَفر والنازح ليس ب هاكر

شارع زفت فقطاع خيم فشارع زفت
قطاع خيم فشارع زفت فقطاع خيم
شارع زفت فقطاع خيم فشارع زفت

خطأ
خطأ
خطأ

عزيزي المستهلك:
تعذّر التعرّفُ على البلد المنتج للحرب

Muddy street, then tent block, then muddy street

The wind in your tent is just an ascetic Sufi mocking you with each whirl

Tent block, then muddy street, then tent block

With his ration card held tight in his extended hand
The IDP walks along the streets searching
Like a mine detector

Muddy street, then tent block, then muddy street

A tomato vendor: If only there were a tomato festival, so that people could
    learn to associate
  the color red with something else

Tent block, muddy street, then tent block

An onion vendor: Long live life!
An eggplant vendor: Ha ha ha!

Tent block, then muddy street, then tent block

Life in the camp is encrypted despair, but the IDPs are not hackers

Muddy street, then tent block, then muddy street
Tent block, then muddy street, then tent block
Muddy street, then tent block, then muddy street

ERROR
ERROR
ERROR

Dear consumer—

Could not identify the producer of war!

في روضة أطفال المخيم

في روضة أطفال المخيم
طلبت ان يرسم كل منهم شيئا ناقصا من هذا العالم
كل واحد منهم رسم نفسه!
في روضة أطفال المخيم
طلبت محو شيء من هذا العالم، اتفقوا رغم انف عراكهم اليومي،
من كل أطرافه وبأقل من لتر واحد من الدموع محوا العالم!

*

طلبت منهم أن يختاروا اغنية لنغني معا بأصواتنا المزعجة
قال كلهم «أريد أن أكون»
ولأنني استقبل الأشياء بطريقة خاطئة حينما اتعثر، هززت رأسي ورددت لم يتم وضع لحن على قصيدة آن
سيكستون «أريد أن اموت» لحد الآن ورسمت ابتسامة زائفة،
ثم فشلت في إيجاد صوتي ثانية

*

اليوم واثناء زيارة سفير اليونيسيف (الذي لم أتأكد من نواياه) للروضة
سأل الأطفال عما يعوزونه
طلبوا متفقين على رأي واحد «بذلات برتقالية»
كي ينبشوا أكياس الزبالة بحرية دون أن يزعجهم مراعس الأمن بطلب حصة مما يعثرون عليه من قطع
حلوى رميت عن طريق الخطأ،
اليوم وزعنا الحلوى عليهم،
قام كل منهم برمي القطعة خاصته في كيس زبالة،
وراح ينبش عن حلمه المتآكل!

In the Camp's Kindergarten

In the camp's kindergarten
I asked each child to draw something missing from this world
Each one of them drew themselves!
In the camp's kindergarten
I asked them to erase something from this world
And they agreed despite their daily struggles
From every side
With less than a single liter of tears,
They erased the world!

*

I asked them to choose a song for us to sing together in our annoying voices
Everyone said, "Wanting to Be"
They tripped me up, I shook my head
Replied that Anne Sexton had not yet put
"Wanting to Die" to music
I painted a fake smile on my face
Then failed once more to find my voice!

*

Today, when the UNICEF ambassador
(whose intentions I have not confirmed)
Visited the kindergarten
He asked the children what they hoped for
Unanimously, they requested the orange uniforms of street sweepers
So they could search through garbage bags freely
Without being bothered by those policing their dumpster diving
Demanding a portion when they find pieces of candy thrown away by mistake
Today we distributed candy to them
Each of them tossed their piece into a garbage bag
Then went digging for their eroded dreams!

قصيدتان في قصيدة ناقصة

لكل خمسون مدينة هدمت في البلاد قصيدة فارغة كالبلاد

ولكل مخيم يبنى قصيدة أطول من مدى الصاروخ

أعمق من بئر النسيان الذي لا نحظى بالوقوع فيه

أوسع من فرج ساشا غري الأقرب لعيون النازحين طوال الوقت

اسمحوا لي برعشة

أعرض من الفضاء الذي احتلته رائحة إبطيٌ سافين

شهقة عميــــــــــــيقة وسأرجع

أكبر من الأرض

أجرأ من لسان يشتم مدير المخيم

ألطف من أصبعي الوسطى التي تنتصب بوجه الجميع كلما سمعتُ

كلمة حياة

أخف من كلمة هاي تخرج من فم قحبة

أكثر ملأً بالمعنى من مقبرة

أبسط من نصب خيمة، أكثر تعقيدا من التنفس فيها

Two Poems in an Incomplete Poem

For every fifty destroyed towns in this country, there is a poem as empty as
the country
And for every camp built, a long poem, longer than the range of a missile
Deeper than the well of oblivion, which we never get to fall into
Wider than Sasha Grey's vagina, which is closer to the eyes of
IDPs than anything else
Let me tremble—
Broader than the space occupied by the stench of Safeen's armpits
A deeeeeep breath and I will return
Larger than the earth
Bolder than a tongue insulting the camp manager
Kinder than my middle finger, which still rises toward the world whenever I
hear the word life
And lighter than the *hi* from a prostitute's mouth
Filled with more meaning than a cemetery
Simpler than pitching a tent, more complicated than breathing in it

أخبار عابرة

DAILY MAIL: SAS troops find severed heads of 50 Yazidi sex slaves as they close in . . .

مائة أذن؛ مائة قرط وصراخ وصوت الصم

مائة عين؛ حزمات رموش وسنوات من النظر

مائة منخر؛ اختناق بالأوكسجين

مائة خد؛ مختبرات لصفعات التجارب والصفعات تتكاثر كالفئران

مائة شفة؛ نسيان القبلة ونسيان الماء وسجن اللغة

ألف وأربعمائة سن؛ نفي العقل، ألف وأربعمائة سنة

هل هذا ما تعنونه بخمسين رأس؟

Ephemeral News

DAILY MAIL: SAS troops find severed heads of 50 Yazidi sex slaves as they close in . . .

One hundred ears: one hundred earrings and shrieks and the voice of the
deaf

One hundred eyes: bundles of eyelashes and years of vision

One hundred nostrils: suffocation by oxygen

One hundred cheeks: labs for experimental slaps—and the slaps proliferate
like rats

One hundred lips: forgetting kisses and forgetting water and imprisoning
language

One thousand four hundred teeth: the denial of reason, one thousand four
hundred years

Is this what you mean by fifty heads?

Dara Deqan

laşê te dareke deqa ye
lêkhatî, pêkhatî ji
şîrê dayikên tu jê re bûyî pîrik
û teniya beroşêd xwanêd miriyêd
te xerîbî li ser gêrrayî
bi şewat,
bê tebat te distiriya, hevîrek
ji ava destê sibê, ji genimê firikî li hingurêd êvara
te xwanê bîr û bîranînê li ber çermê xwe kir
te xwanê pîşeyê ji destê xwe li ber destê xwe kir

Tree of Tattoos

your body a tree of tattoos
made with
milk from women who called you midwife
soot from cauldrons of funeral feasts
for villagers you lamented
you kneaded the water of dawn
into the flour of dusk
to feed your skin memory
to feed your hand craft

Translated from Kurmanji by the poet

Of Body, Distance, & Metaphor

We carry the river, its body of water, in our body.
Natalie Diaz

I was conceived in the land between two rivers, Navava
My grandmother named her sister Navava
And named my niece Xunav, *dew*
Xun, *blood*
Av, *water*
Then she died of thirst
On a dry mountain with a dewy memory in Navava
I was too dry to weep then
And now these words dry my body up

The Tigris and Euphrates are still running in abundance in the Book of
    Genesis
Still running in abundance
In our songs and prayers, vehicles of despair
Drying up before our eyes

My grandmother visits me in my sleep
How is life in Amreeka, my little daughter? she asks
It's wonderful, I say, *you know, Mountain Dew is bottled up*

As I piss in the morning, I open a new tab on Safari:
Daughter, in America the river isn't wet.
Young girls learn to fill their jugs on the internet.
A Pashto mother tells her daughter in a landay

In Kurmanji, we say *my womb tongue*
Instead of *my mother tongue*

In my womb tongue
Pêxem, *a message*, breaks into *grief-on-feet*
Pêxember, *a messenger, grief-on-feet-forward*
To say *wind*, just set air free from your insides—ba
Ba, the autobiography of wind
Ba—your mouth, a yawing word pit
A song slithers away from
Songs, our coded grief—on feet, of wind
O xerîbo, bayê xerbî xema tînê
O stranger, running east, western winds carry
Bitter memories from our pastlands
The song slithers

It is low tide this morning
High tide this afternoon, the tidelog shows
On the ferry to San Francisco
I open *Lunario sentimental*, Lugones writes:
Every word is a dead metaphor.

In my womb tongue, laş, *body*, breaks into *in-motion*—
River, wind, word.

Wacida Xêro

is a poet, singer, multi-instrumentalist, music and language teacher, and community organizer. In the wake of the 2014 genocide, she became a refugee at Newroz Camp in Rojava, the Autonomous Administration of North and East Syria, where she advanced her studies in music in community with the refugees. She's now the lead singer for the band Mîrzo, as well as a singer in Koral Mesopotamia, a project of the Goethe-Institut in Iraq. She lives in the city of Shingal and performs regularly across Iraq.

li 'esiriyeke teng ji 'esiriyêd ber îvara

li 'esiriyeke teng ji 'esiriyêd ber îvara
çiqilêd dareke hêjîra û dareke hinara
lê bilind bilind, li qulîçka hewşa cînara
lê ji du kokêd cuda, herro
xwe lêk dipîçin li ser dîwara
tazî li hembêza yekûdu
li ser devê du riya
li ber çavê xwedê û rêbwara

late one tapering afternoon

late one tapering afternoon
from two discrete tap roots
a fig tree and a pomegranate tree
grow high up over the walls
at the corner of a neighbor's yard
their branches writhe
naked embracing
at the mouth of an intersection
in the sight of god and passersby

Ewrên bê Xîreta

Çilo ewrên payizê bi ewrên bêxîreta hatîne bi navkirin?

Demsal payse nuhe, ewrên baran jî carna bi ser me de digirin.

Em jî ji xanî û hewşa derketîne û li dinyayê dinêrin.

Em destêt xwe lêk diferkînin, destêt me kirkvî ne û em jî dibîjine yekûdo
   wûûûûû destêt me çi hişkbûyne.

Dûra em li xwe vedgêrin dibîjin xwe: dê xwete baran bê wê nerimbin.

Lingêt me jî bê gore dicemidin. Carna em xwe bi gore dikin, û milêt me jî, lê
   em destêt xwe lêk

dipîçin û dikin biçenkêt xwe û li hîviya baranê ne lêk kombûyî ne.

Sebrê me li xanî û hewşa de nayê.

Ji xwe zarwa hederê xwe kirîne ji nuhe de. Cilkêt zivistanê li ber xwe kirîne û
   xwe li ber derê

hewşê hiltavîjin da baran bê û xwe li ber şilkin.

Heçiyê ji wan jina çav li zarwêt xwe dikevê nifirekê lî dike dibîjê:

Quzdak, pa yek li ber we re dighê?

Pa heke hûn cemidîn û we xwe bi ser me de giriyan xwedê ji we bir.

Her ew dikenin û li şare'êde bazdidin û dibîjine dakêt xwe: guhmedê . . .
   medê

Daka mi û cînarêt xwe li civata yek li ber derê hewşê rûniştîne û ji xafilde
   dinya bi ewir digeriyê

da bibe baran, mi dî daka mi got: ele ewrên bêxîreta wî bi ser me de digirin
   û xwe

kenandin gotine yekûdu: erê xwedê heye raste.

Heke wisa got, hate bîra mi berî çend roja ez li mala hevale xwe bûm û daka
   wê jî digot ewrêt bêxîreta wî girte ser me.

Lê hî ez nizanim çima wisa dibîjin, nû vêce ez wî pirs ji daka xwe dikim: Da,
   çima hûn dibîjin ewrên bêxîreta?

Got: berê wextê mal û xaniyêt me axînbûn

Hersal hêswan û hewran jî re diviya û heke dilopkiriban me ser jî dihêswa,

The Lazybones' Clouds

Who first called fall clouds *the lazybones' clouds*?
The season has turned, fall rain clouds close in.
We step out of the house, the yard, to watch.
Our hands tremble. We rub them together. We turn to each other and say,
    Hoowee! Our hands are frozen stiff.
Later, on our own, we console ourselves: *It's about to rain, our hands should*
    thaw out.
Our bare feet freeze. And our shoulders. We pull socks on. We wring the
    cold from our hands then tuck them under our armpits and gather to
    wait for the rain.
In our home and our yards, we grow impatient.
Children seem to be the most prepared. Already in their winter sweaters.
    They horse around in the street, waiting for the rain to wash them clean.
Any decent mother catching sight of her child outside curses him out:
You little mothercunt! Who let you off leash?
If you get a cold and come crying to me: God help you.
And the children just laugh and horse around some more in the street,
    shouting back to their mothers: *Turn a deaf ear! . . . a deaf ear!*
My mother and her neighbors drift to the same house and pop a squat just
    outside the gate and as dark rain clouds roll in over the world, I hear the
    mothers' chorus. The lazybones' clouds rumble. They force laughter.
    One says, *God almighty!*, the other, *You got that right.*
In their voices, I heard my friend's mother, a couple days back, crying out,
    The lazybones' clouds are closing in on us.
A phrase I still don't understand, so I ask my own mother: *Ma, why lazybones?*
In the past, every house and home was adobe.
Each year, before the cold set in and the snows came, each house needed to
    be repaired and replastered so they wouldn't spring a leak.
But some families lazed about deep into the fall, until the clouds closed in.

hîj zû berî berf û sermayê.

Lê pa hinek kes bêxîretbûn, piştî dibû payiz û ev çaxê salê ewrên payzê digir-
tin ser nû bi xwe

dihisyan û radbûn daw û dîlêt xwe bi ber xwe ve dikirin, heriya xwe diceblan-
din û dest bi hêswana mal û xaniyên xwe dikirin.

Vêce ha ji ber wêkê digotin ewrên bê xîreta.

As the first drops fell, they'd rush around, rucking up their long skirts, rolling up their long sleeves, mixing up their clay and slathering it onto house and home.

So, the lazybones' clouds.

Têgehiştina Zaroka

Xwarzîka mina pêncsalî
Ji ronahiya derî de tê
Ku boqeke pîvaza li ber mamê min de dimînê kuxka wî birûskî
"Werin, werin, ejdehayekî avreşok li baxê me de ye"
Hîj pitata xwe dicûm weke golikekî nuhatî, ez xwe çend dikim da bibînim
"Kanî?" ez çavêd xwe digêrim û dipirsim.
Destê xwe li sonda hişîn de tînê û li min direşînê
Ez xwe çend dikim zikê xanî û li pî xwe derî pîve didim.

A Child's Perception

My five-year-old niece
ripples in the light of the doorway
while my uncle chokes on the stem of a green onion.
"Come see, come see, we have a water dragon in our garden," she says.
My uncle's cough thunders.
I jump up to see, chewing on a potato wedge like a contented calf.
"Where is it?" I ask, looking around.
She grabs the green hose and sprays me.
I jump back into the house and slam the door shut.

Acknowledgments

Thanks to the editors of Harriet (Poetry Foundation), for publishing Shook's essay "Bar Codes and Mass Graves: A Reading by Seven Emerging Êzîdî Poets," which contained excerpts of earlier versions of translations of poems by Emad Bashar, Jaff, Saad Shivan, and Zêdan Xelef.

Thanks to the editors of *Spoon River Poetry Review* for publishing earlier versions of Emad Bashar's "(cell)," "Drowning," and "The Knight."

Thanks to the editors of *Conjunctions* and *World Literature Today*, as well as the publishing houses Kashkul Books and Gato Negro Ediciones, for publishing Zêdan Xelef's poetry, sometimes in earlier versions.

Thanks to Dr. Rachel Dbeis for her expertise in Arabic. Thanks to Will Evans for his vision and enthusiasm. Thanks to Linda Stack-Nelson for their patience and keen eyes.

Editor/Translator Biographical Information

Bryar Bajalan is a writer, translator, and filmmaker currently pursuing a doctorate in Arabic and Islamic Studies at the University of Exeter. His work has appeared in *Ambit*, *Hyperallergic*, and *Modern Poetry in Translation*, among others. His short documentary about early twentieth-century Baghdadi poet Al-Zahawi won an award for outstanding achievement at the Tagore International Film Festival. With Shook, he has cotranslated Al-Saddiq Al-Raddi's *A Friends Kitchen* (Poetry Translation Centre, 2023) and Zêdan Xelef's *A Barcode Scanner* (Kashkul Books, 2021/Gato Negro Ediciones, 2022). Bajalan currently directs The House of Maqam, a major oral history project documenting the musical legacy of Mosul, where he also served as a Principal Investigator for the oral history archive Mosul Lives and as a producer for the live album *Mosul Live* (Rare Bird/Unnamed Press, 2024).

Alana Marie Levinson-LaBrosse is a poet, translator, and assistant professor at the American University of Iraq, Sulaimani (AUIS). She earned her Ph.D. in Kurdish Studies at the University of Exeter, specializing in nineteenth-century poetry, and holds an M.F.A. from Warren Wilson College as well as an M.Ed. from the University of Virginia. Her debut collection, *Dream State*, will appear from Unnamed Press in 2025. Her writing has appeared in *Modern Poetry in Translation*, *World Literature Today*, *In Other Words*, *Plume*, *Epiphany*, *Sewanee Review*, the *Iowa Review*, and *Words Without Borders*. Her book-length works include Kajal Ahmed's *Handful of Salt* (2016), Abdulla Pashew's *Dictionary of Midnight* (2019), Nali's *My Moon Is the Only Moon* (2021) and Farhad Pirbal's *The Potato Eaters* (2024). She serves as the Founding Director of Kashkul and was the Founding Director of the Slemani UNESCO City of Literature. She is a 2022 NEA Fellow, the first ever working from the Kurdish.

Shook is a poet and translator based in California. Their most recent book-length translations include Mikeas Sánchez's *How to Be a Good Savage* (Milkweed Editions, 2024) with Wendy Call, Conceição Lima's *No Gods Live Here* (Deep Vellum, 2024), Alfonso Ochoa and Azul López's *Giant on the Shore* (Transit Children Editions, 2024), Farhad Pirbal's *Refugee Number 33,333* (Deep Vellum, 2024) with Pshtiwan Babakr, Jorge Carlos Fonseca's *Pigs in Delirium* (Insert Press, 2024), and Víctor Terán's *The Thorn of Your Name* (Poetry Translation Centre, 2024). Shook has collaborated with numerous translators to introduce over twenty Kurdish writers into both English and Spanish.

Zêdan Xelef is a poet, translator, archivist, and culture preservationist. They were born on a farm near the confluence of the Tigris and Khabour rivers on the Iraq-Syria border, where they waved at the departing trains with the first light of the day. They grew up in the village of Izêr on the south side of Shingal mountain, where they herded four goats along with three of their cousins. They are the author of *A Barcode Scanner* (Kashkul Books, 2021/ Gato Negro Ediciones, 2022), poems written in and about Chammishkko Camp, where they lived with their family for five years after being displaced from their village in the wake of the 2014 Yazidi genocide perpetrated by the Islamic State. The title poem of the book was adapted into a poetry film by Shook and received the Award for Best Film for Tolerance at the 2020 ZEBRA Poetry Film Festival in Berlin. Xelef's poetry and translations have appeared in numerous literary outlets, including the *Los Angeles Review of Books, World*

Literature Today, Poetry London, Tripwire, Conjunctions, and *Poetry.* Their selection and translation of Selim Temo's poems, in collaboration with Alana Marie Levinson-LaBrosse, came out under the title *Nightlands* from Pinsapo Press in 2024. They currently live and write in Oakland, California.

Printed in the USA
CPSIA information can be obtained
at www.ICGtesting.com
JSHW020744300724
67277JS00002B/5